WHEELS **THE HISTORY OF LAND TRANSPORT**

TRAINS

David Jefferis

Franklin Watts

London New York Toronto Sydney

Illustrated by
Robert and Rhoda Burns
Chris Forsey
Terry Hadler
Ron Jobson
Michael Roffe

Photographs supplied by
Ace Photo Agency
Mary Evans Picture Library
David Jefferis
Quadrant/Canning Goldrich

Technical consultant
Patrick Devereux

© 1991 Franklin Watts

Franklin Watts
96 Leonard Street
London EC2A 4RH

Published in the
United States by
Franklin Watts Inc.
387 Park Avenue South
New York NY 10016

Published in Australia by
Franklin Watts Australia
14 Mars Road
Lane Cove
NSW 2066

ISBN 0 7496 0475 1

A CIP catalogue record for
this book is available from
the British Library

Printed in Belgium

TRAINS

Contents

Introduction

Railways as we know them today started with the invention of the steam engine. But the idea of using a permanent track to guide wheeled vehicles was thought of long before.

The earliest known trackways date back more than 4,000 years. In Greece, remains still exist of lines of stone blocks, with grooves cut down the middle to act as guides for wheels. By the 1600s, railways were built in parts of Europe, to take minerals from mine workings. The rails were usually of wood – the first metal rails were not laid until 1787, at a coal mine in Sheffield, England. The new metal rails were tougher and stronger than those made of wood, so they could take heavier loads and lasted far longer.

The first steam locomotives were invented in the early 19th century, and by the 1850s, much of the world was gripped by "railway fever", as builders raced to complete thousands of new lines. The train was the king of high speed travel, and remained so until after World War II, when the automobile and aeroplane seriously challenged the dominance of the railways. In many countries, railways have been in decline since the 1950s, but problems of traffic pollution and road congestion have encouraged the development of a new breed of supertrain, able to outrun motorway traffic easily and even, over distances of a few hundred kilometres, beat the airlines at their own game. The future of the railways now looks very bright indeed.

◁ Steam power ruled the railways for a century and a half. In countries where steam trains no longer operate on main line services, preservation societies have sprung up, supported by the time and effort of rail enthusiasts. This old steamer is on a line in California that runs regular services on a short stretch of track.

Speed on rails

These two locomotives span a period of over 160 years. Apart from the fact that they both run on rails, they have little in common except that they are both record breakers of their time. The *Rocket* won a set of steam locomotive trials in 1829; the TGV established a 1990 speed record of 515 km/h (320 mph).

The *Rocket* 1829

▷ The *Rocket* was one of the most successful early locomotives and was capable of nearly 48 km/h (30 mph). Its front-mounted driving wheels had spokes and rims made of wood, with tyres and hubs of metal. The tender carried coal and water.

TGV 1990

▽ The electric-powered Train à Grande Vitesse (TGV) regularly achieves speeds of over 300 km/h (186 mph) on routes in France. The outright rail speed record is currently 515.3 km/h (320.2 mph), achieved by a TGV on a special run in May, 1990.

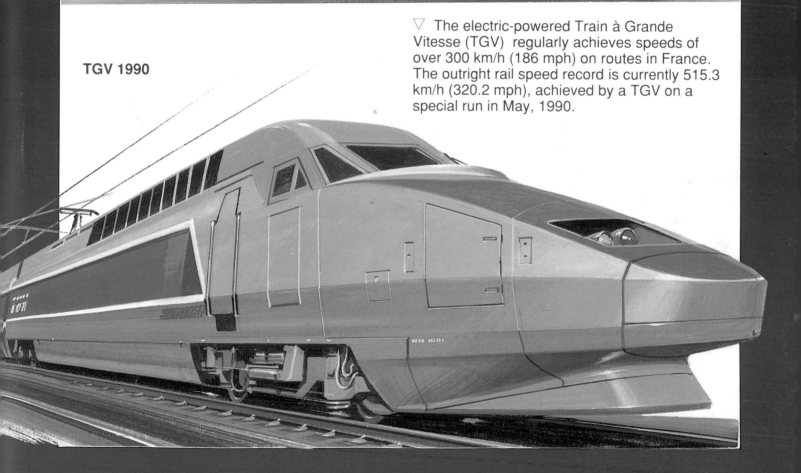

Rail pioneers

All the early rail lines used people or horses to pull the loads. It was not until after the invention of the steam engine by British engineer James Watt in 1774 that the idea of a machine to compete with muscle power was taken seriously.

The first steam locomotive was invented by Richard Trevithick, a Cornish engineer, for use in the Pen-y-Daren ironworks in South Wales. In 1804, the 5-tonne machine started work, but its weight proved too much for the cast-iron rails of the iron-works. Three years later, Trevithick tried to make his invention popular by running another locomotive, *Catch me who can,* on a circular track in London. People paid to see the machine puffing round the track; the bravest rode on its single carriage. But the machine was regarded by most as little more than a fairground toy and Trevithick soon abandoned work on his locomotives.

George Stephenson was a much more successful rail pioneer. His first locomotive ran in 1813. It was for use in mines, and could haul a 30-tonne load of coal at walking pace. Stephenson went on to build a new railway line between the towns of Stockton and Darlington in northern England. The first train was 28 wagons long, with a special carriage for passengers in the middle. This train was hauled by Stephenson's engine, the *Locomotion,* on 27 September 1825. It was a great success, achieving speeds of 32 km/h (20 mph). Even so, for some time after the opening, passenger trains did not use steam engines. People were suspicious of the noisy machines and preferred to be pulled by horse, a familiar, if slower means of propulsion. Over the years Stephenson and his son, Robert, went on to build many other successful railway lines.

▽ On 21 February 1804, Trevithick's locomotive hauled a heavy load of iron to win a wager. The 70 men who climbed aboard for the 16 km (10 mile) run became the first people to travel on a train pulled by steam.

6

△ Stephenson's *Locomotion* hauling its first load of passengers. On this train there was just one proper passenger carriage – most people sat in wagons.

▷ French inventor Marc Séguin's 1829 engine, built for the St Etienne to Lyons rail company. The engine had a multi-tube boiler, an arrangement which allowed heat from the firebox to pass along 43 thin tubes before reaching the chimney. The tubes were immersed in water, and heated it evenly and quickly to boiling point. The steam thus raised was fed to a vertical cylinder on each side, pushing a piston up and down. Each piston was joined to the driving wheels by metal connecting rods, allowing them to turn smoothly, so driving the engine along the track.

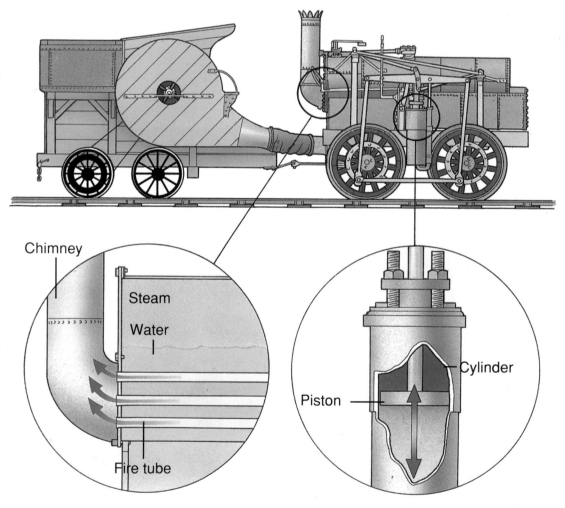

Chimney

Steam

Water

Fire tube

Piston

Cylinder

△ In this diagram you can see how the fire tubes passed through the boiler water before reaching the chimney. Steam from the heated water collected in the top of the boiler.

△ Each piston moved up and down in its cylinder, one on each side of the engine.

Rocket on rails

The week beginning 5 October 1829 marked a dramatic trial between a number of locomotives. Their builders were competing for a production contract for the new Leeds and Manchester railway. The rules of the Rainhill trials demanded many runs, at an average speed of at least 16 km/h (10 mph), with locomotives powerful enough to pull a load of at least three times their own weight.

Inventors and designers of the day offered a variety of machinery, including the horse-powered *Cycloped*, and even a man-powered machine. But the serious entries were powered by steam. They were the *Rocket, Novelty* and *Sans Pareil*. On the first day of the trials, 10,000 spectators lined the 2.8 km (1.75 mile) route, eagerly watching the trains make steadily faster and faster runs. On the first day the top speeds of the steam locomotives hit 45 km/h (28 mph). The horse-powered *Cycloped* did less well, hauling wagons carrying 50 people at the less than impressive speed of 8 km/h (5 mph). The man-powered machine made an even worse showing – its two-man crew puffed and panted as they pulled six passengers at a steady walking pace. From here on, the trials belonged to the steam locomotives.

During the tests, faults and failures took their toll. *Sans Pareil* had a failed water pump and *Novelty* blew a boiler joint. Only the *Rocket* put in a steady and reliable performance. When the judges added up the scores, *Rocket* was declared the winner. A £500 prize and the business of building the new railway's locomotives went to *Rocket*'s makers, George and Robert Stephenson and their partner, Henry Booth.

Keeping on track

Early rail equipment had used ordinary wheels, either running in specially dug ruts, or on flanged track. By the time of the Rainhill trials, the most advanced trains used flanged wheels, rolling on metal rails. The flanges kept locomotives and carriages safely on course, enabling them to go round curves smoothly. Today's trains use much the same system.

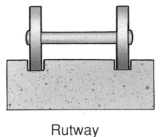

Rutway

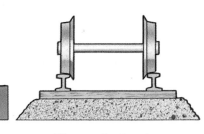

Flanged track

Flanged wheels

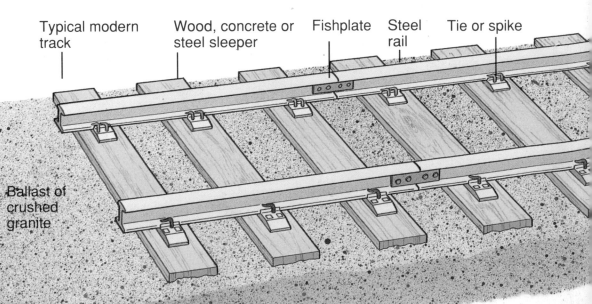

Typical modern track

Wood, concrete or steel sleeper

Fishplate

Steel rail

Tie or spike

Ballast of crushed granite

Competitors at the Rainhill Locomotive trials

△ *Sans Pareil* (a French name meaning "without rival") was the biggest locomotive.

△ *Novelty* was the lightweight entry.

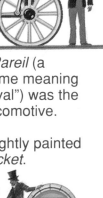

▽ The brightly painted yellow *Rocket*.

▽ The *Cycloped* had a horse as "engine".

△ The iron firebox of the *Rocket* was strongly made, with massive rivets. The pipes were made of copper or brass.

△ One of *Rocket*'s driving wheels and the connecting rod. The wheels were made of wood, with metal hubs and flanged tyres.

Railway builders

△ An American locomotive thunders across a bridge in the Rocky Mountains.

Just eight years after the opening of the Liverpool and Manchester railway, more than 2,900 km (1,800 miles) of track had been completed in Great Britain alone. Around the world, the railway business boomed as more and more countries joined in the race for better transportation.

Building rail routes was neither easy nor cheap. To avoid steep gradients, cuttings and embankments had to be made. Tunnels and bridges were built to cross mountains and rivers. All had to be finished before a single train could run. Builders often got a bad name for constructing poor quality tracks, but, particularly on difficult routes,

the idea was to get a line, any line, in operation as quickly as possible. It could be gradually improved later, when the money was rolling in from freight and passenger operations.

Among the most famous long-distance routes was the American transcontinental link, built across deserts and mountains between 1863 and 1869. Construction workers from the Union Pacific and Central Pacific Railroads worked from east and west, their aim to join the tracks at the halfway point, in the state of Utah. Life was tough as the workers had to lay up to 16 km (10 miles) of track a day. In the Rocky Mountains, the line was blasted

△ Railway bridges and tunnels were often impressive stuctures. Scotland's Forth Bridge, opened in 1890, remains the most massive iron rail bridge in the world.

from solid rock, and deaths from falling rock or mistimed gunpowder blasts were common. There were attacks from native American warriors and flash floods washed away newly-constructed bridges. Disease and death were caused by inhaling rock dust and explosive fumes or by exhaustion.

When the two lines neared each other, instead of joining up, they went straight past, building the lines side by side! The exact joining point had not been agreed, and the companies were receiving government money for laying the line. They were officially stopped only after 362 km (225 miles) of parallel track had been laid. The "golden spike", the last fixing pin on the line, was finally driven home on 10 May 1869. The new railway was 2,776 km (1,725 miles) long.

Rail around the world

Africa
The first line was from Alexandria to Cairo. The 208 km (129 mile) track opened in 1856.

Asia
In April 1853 a line was opened between the Indian cities of Bombay and Thana.

Japan's rail system opened in 1872, with a line from Yokohama to Sinegawa.

Australia
In 1855, a short line from Flinders Street to Sandridge introduced Australia's first steam service. Earlier tracks had included an 8 km (5 mile) line in Tasmania, on which trucks were pushed by convicts.

△ Germany's first railway of 1835.

Europe
Among the earliest lines was Belgium's Brussels to Malines line, opened in 1835.

The first public steam rail service in France ran in 1837, from Paris to the town of Le Pecq.

North America
The first steam locomotive in North America was the 1825 machine built by John Stevens.

Canada's first steam railway was opened in 1832. It ran between the St Lawrence and Richelieu rivers, a distance of 26.5 km (16.5 miles).

▽ An American engine of 1831.

The golden age of rail

In the 19th century, the spreading railway network changed the way people lived, often in most unexpected ways.

In pre-railway days, food shortages were common, and moving supplies any great distance was slow and expensive. For example, wheat bought in the south of France, where it was grown, cost a quarter the price it fetched in Paris. With the coming of the railways, such huge price differences were removed; the additional costs of rail transport were quite low.

In Switzerland the first railway was nicknamed the "bread train", since it brought a supply of fresh rolls every morning to the people of Zurich. Other fresh foods became available to city dwellers, often for the first time. These included milk brought direct from farms in the countryside, newly caught fish, and freshly picked fruit and vegetables. By the 1860s, even poor families in the cities could add fresh vegetables to the dinner table.

Foods like these had to be kept cool while they were being taken to market. As refrigerators had not yet been invented, large quantities of ice were used. Ice making became a boom industry. It was hacked out of frozen lakes in places which had severe winters. In warmer parts, such as California, teams were sent up mountains to bring back huge chunks of ice from the highest peaks.

Another great change created by the railways was the adventure of travel. Before trains, few ordinary people ever left their home towns. Now it was possible to explore the world beyond your immediate neighbourhood. At first, only the rich could afford such journeys, but soon cheap-rate excursions were being organised, a tradition which continues today, both on the railways and in the air.

19th-century high technology

The railways were the leading edge of technological development in the 19th century, the Victorian equivalent of today's supersonic jets. Apart from the trains themselves, new and improved services, comforts and luxuries were added continually, as privately owned rail companies battled with each other to gain business and make bigger profits.

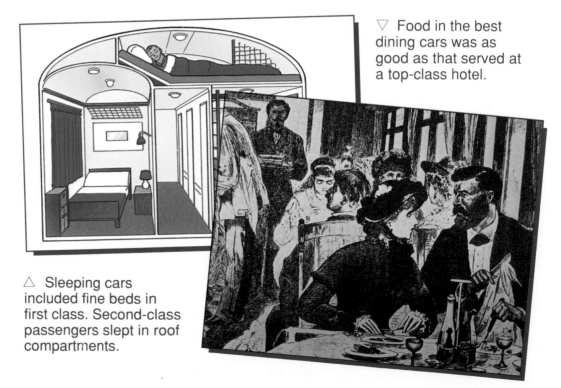

▽ Food in the best dining cars was as good as that served at a top-class hotel.

△ Sleeping cars included fine beds in first class. Second-class passengers slept in roof compartments.

Gauges big and small

A track's gauge is the width between the rails. There are three types of gauge: narrow, standard and broad. Widths vary widely within each category of gauge.

Standard gauge is the most widely used, at 1.435 m (4 ft 8½ in).

Broad gauge was a competitor to standard gauge, especially in the 19th century. Enthusiasts claimed the extra width gave more room for passengers and gave a better ride.

Narrow gauge

△ This 260 mm (10¼ in) gauge locomotive runs on England's Wells and Walsingham light railway. It is the most powerful engine of its size in the world.

Standard gauge

△ Standard gauge is by far the most common, and is in use by most countries in the world today. The locomotive shown is an express of the 1870s.

Broad gauge

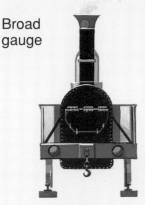

△ The widest broad gauge was 2.134 m (7 ft). Today's widest gauge is 1.676 m (5 ft 6 in), used in several countries including India and Argentina.

◁ Mail went by train. Letter sorting was carried out in special mail coaches while on the move.

△ Signalmen controlled rail traffic from signal boxes like this. Everything was operated by hand.

Faster and faster

Speed was the main factor behind the successful development of the railways. Quite simply, people were willing to pay for rapid transport. So, throughout the 19th century, locomotive designers and railway companies battled to be first with the fastest services. In the 1820s, 50 km/h (31 mph) was considered an impressive top speed. By the 1890s, the most powerful express trains were touching 160 km/h (100 mph) or more.

△ The 1849 6-2-0 Norris engine had giant-size driving wheels, intended to give it an extra turn of speed. The driver had a commanding view from the wooden cab.

▷ On 10 May, 1893, engine number 999 hauled a four-coach train of the Empire State Express at 181 km/h (112.5 mph), to establish a new world speed record. This was the first time *anything* man-made had gone this fast. Later, No. 999 had its driving-wheel size reduced for slower, normal running.

Wheel codes

About 1900, the American Frederick Whyte devised a number code to describe the number of wheels on a locomotive. The first number is for the leading wheels, the second for the driving wheels, the third for the trailing wheels. In addition, many codes have names. Here are some examples.

2-2-0 Planet

2-6-0 Mogul

4-4-0 American

2-10-2 Santa Fe

2-8-2 Mikado

4-6-2 Pacific

4-8-4 Confederation

4-8-8-4 Big Boy

From wooden seats to air-conditioned comfort

During early runs on the Stockton and Darlington railway, people sat in coal trucks to enjoy the ride. But once passenger-carrying became big business, railway companies built proper coaches. Early ones had three classes – first class resembled the stagecoaches of the time, while second class were open with a canopy over the top. Passengers in third class sat in open trucks. Modern coaches vary from commuter "crush class" specials to comfortable business class coaches.

△ This early rail passenger coach was a simple wooden box. Standard stagecoach bodies were often used too. They were mounted onto wagon frames and wheels.

◁ The cutaway view shows three classes of accommodation in a 19th-century passenger coach. The coach is made mostly of wood, on a metal base and wheels.

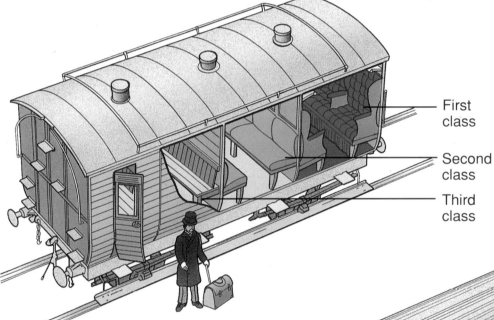

First class

Second class

Third class

▷ A modern high-speed coach is made of lightweight steel. Wheels at either end have a suspension system for a smooth ride and powerful brakes for efficient stopping power. Tinted and double-glazed windows reduce glare and noise. Seats are padded for passengers' comfort.

Adjustable seats

Double-glazed windows

Steel construction

Giants of steam

△ A Union Pacific Big Boy. 201 of these railway giants were built in the 1940s.

The biggest locomotives ever made were the 4-8-8-4 Big Boys built for the American Union Pacific railroad. Complete with tender, a Big Boy weighed over 508 tonnes, and could pull a freight train of more than 5,000 tonnes. When hauling passenger trains, Big Boys roared along at up to 129 km/h (80 mph).

Big American locomotives have mostly had large numbers of wheels, to spread the weight on the light tracks. But when the first Big Boy started work in September 1941, the Union Pacific found that, despite its 4-8-8-4 layout, the weight still made track replacement an urgent necessity, otherwise the existing lightweight rails would have been pounded to pieces.

Garratts were another type of giant steam engine. They came in three jointed sections, which could swivel or articulate, to allow them to travel on tight bends. The first ones were built in 1909 for use on a narrow gauge line on the island of Tasmania, south of Australia. Over the years, about 2,000 Garratts were built, the largest being one made in 1932 for the

16

Russian state rail system. It weighed over 260 tonnes.

Garratts were popular in Africa too. In the 1960s, many of the cabs of South African Garratts were armoured to protect crews from attack by nationalist rebels. The water tanks were made of thinner metal though, and trains often rolled into stations with water spouting out of bullet holes. Further north in Africa, Garratts running in countries such as Zambia and Zimbabwe have had to cope with other dangers. On the 1980 Christmas Day run from Bulawayo to Victoria Falls, a Garratt ploughed into an elephant standing on the line. The locomotive was derailed, while the poor elephant was killed outright.

△ Steam power is still used in some parts of the world. Here an Indian driver stands in front of his giant wide-gauge locomotive. Together with several other countries, including Pakistan, Spain and Argentina, India uses a gauge of 1.676 m (5 ft 6 in).

◁ An articulated Garratt. Cab and boiler are in the middle, tenders at both ends.

Electric trains

Successful as the steam engine was, it was only a matter of time before it was replaced by electricity, a much more efficient source of energy.

Electric power on the railway dates back as far as 1835, when American blacksmith Thomas Davenport ran a miniature engine in the state of Vermont. The first public electric train was German, a service running near Berlin in 1881. The line operated a 26-passenger car along a 2.5 km (1.5 mile) route. But electrifying the railways did not happen overnight, nor are electric locomotives used everywhere today, as building an electric line is expensive. Power is supplied either through an extra third rail, or by an overhead wire "catenary" system, and to be worthwhile, the route has to be busy enough to pay for the cost of installing this expensive equipment.

For routes which do not have enough traffic, there is another solution: the diesel-electric locomotive. This carries its own power station in the form of an oil-fuelled diesel engine, that charges electric motors. These then drive the wheels.

The first successful diesel-electric locomotive was an American ALCO demonstration machine, in service between 1924 and 1925. The production locomotives which followed were used for many years – the first one worked for 32 years before being retired. Also in 1925, the German *Flying Hamburger* became the first high speed diesel-electric train. In tests, it hit a top speed of nearly 200 km/h (124 mph). Diesel-electrics are not as efficient as pure electric engines though, as they have to carry the extra weight of the engine and a heavy tank of diesel oil.

▽ In 1903 this Siemens and Halske electric locomotive attained a record-breaking speed of 210 km/h (130 mph), which it held until 1931.

The Siemens machine had side-mounted collectors for its electricity supply, as the power cables ran along the trackside.

▷ An electric engine takes its power from an overhead wire using a pantograph, or through a third "live" rail. The electricity flows to a transformer, which reduces the current (often 25,000 volts) to 2,000 or less for use in the locomotive. A speed control in the cab changes the voltage to alter speed: the more power, the faster the train goes. A rectifier smooths the power into a steady direct current for the traction motors.

▷ A diesel-electric locomotive uses a large diesel engine, similar to those used in heavy trucks. It is fuelled by oil stored in a tank. The engine powers a main generator, which provides electricity for the traction motors.

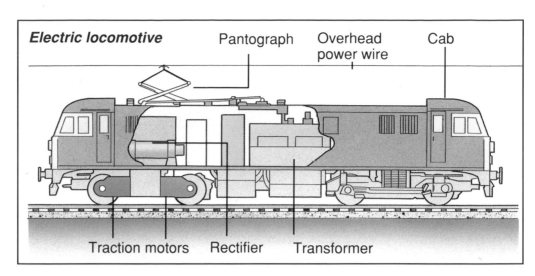

Electric locomotive

Pantograph — Overhead power wire — Cab

Traction motors — Rectifier — Transformer

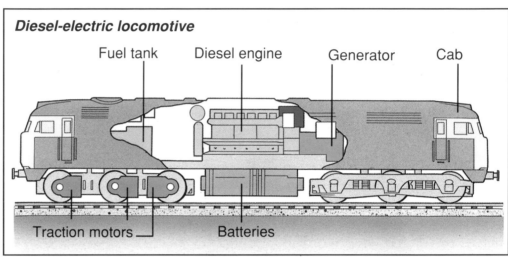

Diesel-electric locomotive

Fuel tank — Diesel engine — Generator — Cab

Traction motors — Batteries

▽ GG1s were smoothly-shaped electric locomotives that were first run by the Pennsylvania Railroad in the 1930s. GG1s hauled trains between New York, Washington and Harrisburg for nearly 40 years.

PENNSYLVANIA 4856

Japan's bullet

In 1965, Japanese technology brought rail transport into a new age. On 1 November, "bullet" trains, named for their speed and appearance, began running on the Shinkansen route between Tokyo and Osaka at an average speed of more than 161 km/h (100 mph), the first scheduled train service in the world to do so.

The Shinkansen line was a new one, built to provide high levels of speed and comfort for passengers. The track was built as straight as possible, with no tight curves to slow the trains down. There are no signals beside the track: instructions are indicated on an instrument panel in the driver's cab. If the driver fails to obey, automatic equipment applies the brakes.

Inside the bullet trains, interiors set new standards for the 1960s, including comfortable airline-style seating and telephones for busy executives. The first passengers on the line were amazed at the quietness of the trains – the windows were double-glazed to keep out the noise.

Travelling by bullet train became so popular that on one extra-busy day in 1975, over 800,000 people were carried. By the end of the following year, no less than a thousand million passengers had travelled on the line.

The success of the Japanese trains started a new fashion in high-speed lines around the world, but one big drawback is the huge cost. Bullet trains run on completely new track, an expensive solution to the problems of travelling at speed. Other countries have tried the cheaper method of improving the suspension of their trains, so they can run nearly as fast, but on the existing track.

△ ▷ Trains running on Japan's Shinkansen ("new network") system fall into two types. High-speed bullet trains like the ones shown above and right are called Hikari ("lightning"); slower expresses are known as Kodama ("echo"). Timetables allow just a 15-second delay during a run.

△ On scenic routes in Japan, these big-windowed trains are used to give panoramic views, ahead as well as to the side, on the way to resort areas.

Tilting trains

Various countries have experimented with tilting trains, with varying degrees of success. The idea is to lean into a bend in much the same way as a cyclist does. This reduces the sideways force felt by the passengers, allowing the train to corner at higher speeds. Italy's Pendulino is a successful modern tilting train, while the French design shown here dates from 1957. Britain's APT-E of the early 1980s failed to live up to its technical promise however, and the sleek prototype is now in a rail museum.

△ APT-E of the early 1980s.

▷ 1957 French tilting train.

The TGV

△ The TGV system requires its own track, with few curves to slow the trains down.

The Train à Grande Vitesse ("high-speed train") is a French trailblazer. The first TGVs started in 1982, on the route from Paris to Lyons, in the south of France. The speed and comfort of these electric trains created a French rail revolution – for the first time on that route, travelling by train was faster than going by air. Jets were quicker when flying, but when you added up the time getting to and from the airport at either end, the total journey worked out longer.

There are now purpose-built TGV lines in other parts of France and more are being added. A recently built section runs from Paris to Rennes. On this route, TGVs cover 373 km (232 miles) in just over two hours, an average speed, including stops, of nearly 3 km (2.75 miles) a minute.

For first-time travellers, a journey on the TGV is an exciting experience. Houses, farms and buildings snap by at lightning speed, while cars on motorways look as if

they are standing still. Comforts on the train include a first-class restaurant, a snack bar, meeting areas, a magazine and newspaper stall, telephones and even a nursery room with bottle warmer and nappy-changing facilities.

Both travellers and drivers love riding the TGV. Unfortunately, so do some criminals, who are attracted by the affluent business people on the train. On one occasion two British travellers were knocked out by crooks armed with an ether-soaked cloth. The passengers were quietly but efficiently robbed as they lay unconscious – to the casual passer-by, they looked as if they were asleep.

To people who don't travel by train, TGVs may be good or bad, depending on where the line is built. In the north of France a new line is welcomed for the valuable trade it brings. In the rich Mediterranean coast area, a new line is regarded as an unnecessary intrusion.

△ The instrument panel in the TGV's driving cab. Speed is controlled by moving the large wheel in front of the driver. Power and speed are indicated on two instruments in front of it. The driver can be in touch with TGV control by radio at any time. The brakes are efficient, but stopping from 290 km/h (180 mph) still takes nearly 3.2 km (2 miles).

▽ Modified versions of the TGV will provide a high-speed link between Britain and France when the world's biggest engineering project, the Channel Tunnel, is completed. Trains will run both ways, in separate tunnels, taking about 35 minutes to complete the 50 km (31 mile) underground run below the sea.

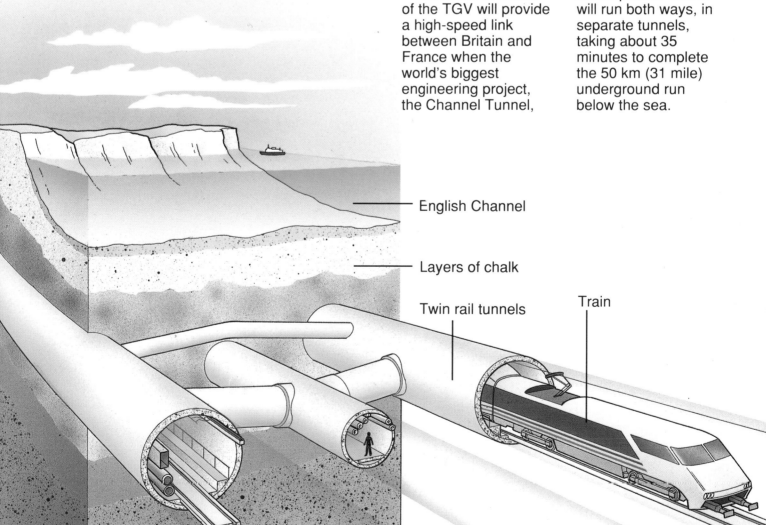

English Channel

Layers of chalk

Twin rail tunnels

Train

Future trains

For the next few years, trains will mostly be updated versions of equipment currently in service. In cities, light rail systems will provide a speedy alternative to riding in cars or buses on congested roads. On long-distance routes, versions of present-day trains such as the TGV will be widely used. The power systems will be better, allowing cheaper running, but top speeds will rise only a little. Around 320 km/h (200 mph) is a practical limit for most routes, except on specially built lines with no sharp bends.

For faster travel, researchers in several countries are developing magnetic levitation or "maglev" designs. Here, powerful magnets raise a train off the ground, and propel it at very high speed along a smooth concrete track. Japan's experimental maglev vehicle has already passed the 500 km/h (310 mph) mark. By 1994, a 43 km (27 mile) test track should be in use, and in the 21st century a link between Tokyo and Osaka could be open for traffic. Using maglev, express train speeds could climb past the 640 km/h (400 mph) mark. Much faster than this though, and trains might have to run in protective tubes, as a collision with a flock of birds or debris at these super-speeds could wreck an entire train.

But however fast and efficient rail travel may become, one thing is for sure: for thousands of people around the world, the old-fashioned "iron horse" steam locomotive will remain king of trains. And preserved steam railways will be run by groups of enthusiasts for as long as the wheels will roll!

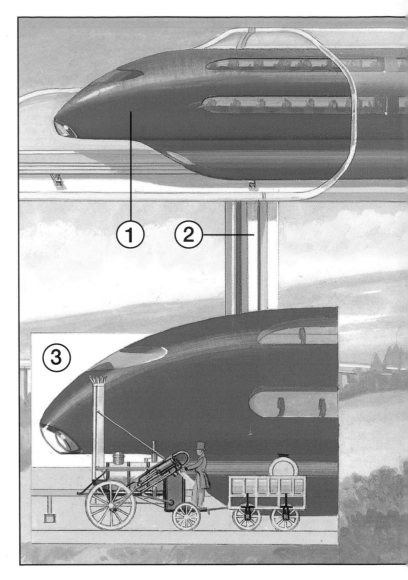

Maglev express, year 2020

This is an idea for an advanced maglev train, designed for high-speed running between major cities in the 21st century. Several key features of the express include:

1 Smoothly-shaped body with specially strengthened front sections designed to withstand the impact of an object hit at high speed.

2 The line is raised above ground where necessary. The track is made as straight as possible to allow the Maglev express to cruise at a speed of around 800 km/h (500 mph).

3 Maglev express and Stephenson's *Rocket*, shown here to the same scale.

4 An enclosing tube may be a necessary protection for the fastest sections of the route. Here we show one such tube, made of super-strong transparent plastic.

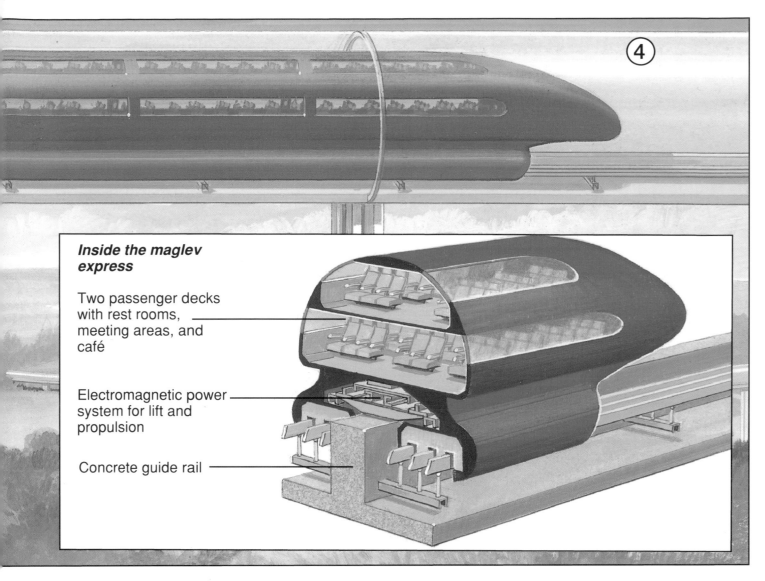

Inside the maglev express

Two passenger decks with rest rooms, meeting areas, and café

Electromagnetic power system for lift and propulsion

Concrete guide rail

◁ The DD1 double-deck city train is based on the ideas of a German designer, Rainer Zimmerman. It would use a single rail system to lift the DD1 above the ground, well clear of any road traffic. The design allows various seating arrangements. For example, the front could be left clear for commuters, while the raised rear section could have lounge seats for passengers wishing to relax and enjoy the view.

Rail progress

These locomotives cover nearly two centuries of railway development. During that time steam power has come and gone, with electricity now the favourite energy supply for almost all new locomotives, large and small.

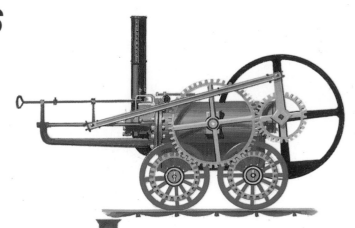

△ **1804 Trevithick's locomotive.** This was the first successful steam locomotive on rails. Its wheels had no flanges – the rails were flanged instead.

▷ **1840s Borsig No. 1.** A 4-2-2 design, this was the first locomotive from the German Borsig works. The design was loosely based on Norris engines of the period.

▷ **1884** *Vittorio-Emanuele II.* The first of a locomotive design that became an Italian classic, built for many years. The type was still in use in the early 1920s.

◁ **1895 Westinghouse electric.** An American design that was the first electric locomotive to haul main-line trains. It collected its power from an overhead line using a pantograph similar to those of today.

△ 1903 *City of Truro.* A British 4-4-0 that could hit 161 km/h (100 mph) in everyday use, not as a one-off stunt such as that of the Empire State Express in 1893.

◁ 1934 Burlington Zephyr. Locomotives pulling this express were the first diesels to have smooth, streamlined body designs. The American Zephyrs regularly achieved top speeds of over 193 km/h (120 mph).

▽ 1938 *Mallard.* This British locomotive smashed the world speed record for steam on 3 July 1938, with a speed of 203 km/h (126 mph). The record stands today.

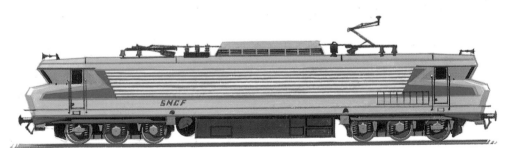

◁ 1970s CC-21000. Before the TGV became the pride of France, these electric locomotives were hauling express trains such as the Mistral at speeds as high as 220 km/h (137 mph).

▷ 1990s ICE. The Inter City Express is Germany's latest high speed train. Unlike the TGV, it can cruise at up to 250 km/h (155 mph) on existing tracks.

Facts and records

Since the dawn of the railways, a fascinating variety of machinery has taken to the tracks. Here are some interesting facts about them and the way in which the world of rail travel has developed over the years.

Richard Trevithick's 1804 Pen-y-Daren locomotive was his second attempt to build such a machine. His first, built for another mine, was not a success.

The Baltimore and Ohio Railroad became the first American rail system to start operations, in 1828.

Belgium's first line, opened in 1835, was the first line opened as part of a national rail network. Others were privately owned tracks, in competition with each other.

By the late 19th century, long-distance routes covered the world. Many luxury passenger services were started, including ones which became famous for their quality of service. These included the Orient Express, which went from Paris to Istanbul. The service ran until 1977. Now the name is owned by a travel company, which sells luxury holidays to Venice. A typical trip includes fine food and wine en route, and the option of returning by Concorde airliner.

The Kruckenberg railcar of 1931 used a diesel engine to spin a rear-mounted propeller. The experimental streamliner took the world speed record at 231 km/h (143.5 mph) in May 1931.

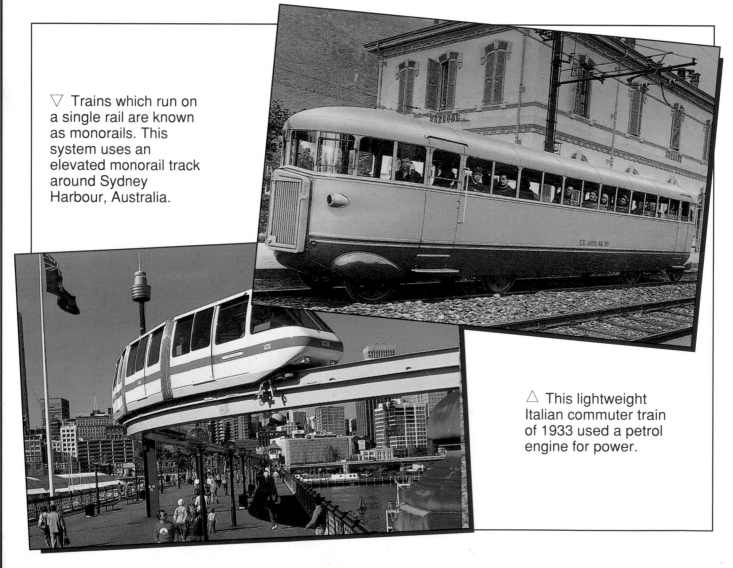

▽ Trains which run on a single rail are known as monorails. This system uses an elevated monorail track around Sydney Harbour, Australia.

△ This lightweight Italian commuter train of 1933 used a petrol engine for power.

The longest rail journey is 9,297 km (5,777 miles), from Moscow to Vladivostok. The Trans-Siberian Express takes a week to cover the distance.

The longest stretch of straight track in the world is across the Nullarbor ("no trees") Plain in Australia. 478 km (297 miles) of the run is in a dead-straight line.

The highest line in the world is in Peru, South America. Here the railway reaches a sky-scraping altitude of 4,817 m (15,806 ft) in the Andes Mountains. A contrast is the Seikan Tunnel in Japan, which burrows 240 m (786 ft) beneath the waves.

Japanese railways take the record for the busiest rail system. The East Japan railway has carried nearly 20 million people in one day.

A curious twin-funnelled train was built by Frenchman Charles Lartigue in the 1880s. It ran on an A-shaped monorail track, which Lartigue intended to be cheap and quick to lay. Lartigue's trains ran in several countries including Ireland, France and Russia. They were not very successful, but since then, monorails have been used in various parts of the world.

The world's largest station is New York's Grand Central Terminal. Its two levels have 67 platforms.

△ Maintaining and running old steam locomotives has become popular in many countries. Here a driver prepares to start off on the footplate of *Joem*, an engine which runs on a short stretch of track in Somerset, England.

▽ The Lartigue monorail system (top), and the Kruckenberg propeller train.

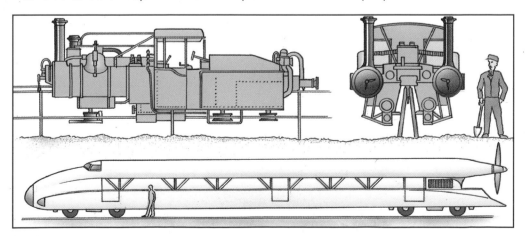

Train technology

This glossary explains many of the technical terms used in this book.

Articulated locomotive
An engine built in two or more sections, that allow it to go round sharper bends than if it were made in one long piece. Among the most famous articulated locomotives are the Garratts used in Africa.

Cutting
Dug-out section through a hill or rise, to allow a railway to pass through. An embankment is a raised section across a ditch or valley. The object, as with a cutting, is to smooth out any steep gradients in the track.

Diesel engine
Engine similar to those used in heavy trucks. Most locomotives use their diesel engines to drive electric motors, but diesel-hydraulic systems use the diesel engine direct, via an oil-filled gear system.

Flange
Lipped edge to the inner side of a train wheel. Flanges on all the wheels keep them centred on the rails and running smoothly.

Footplate
The metal floor of the cab where the driver and fireman of a steam locomotive stand.

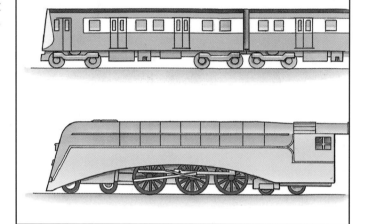

Streamlining
These two trains show the extremes of shape. Top, a square-cut modern commuter diesel; below an express of the 1930s.

Keeping the track level
Steel wheels on steel rails slip easily on steep gradients or in wet weather. So track builders aim for as level a line as possible.

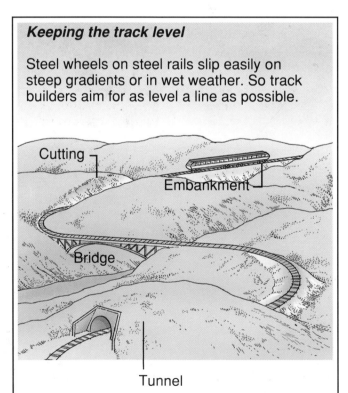

Cutting
Embankment
Bridge
Tunnel

Gauge
Width between the rails. Standard gauge is the most widely used. The loading gauge is used to measure the height and width available on a line. A wagon that is too high or too wide, for example, will not be able to go through a tunnel and would bump against trackside signals.

Maglev
Magnetic levitation. Type of propulsion which uses magnets to lift and speed trains along a guideway, usually a monorail track.

Monorail
A train which runs on a single rail instead of the traditional two.

There are various types of monorail trains, including ones that straddle the top of the rail and those that hang underneath. Future monorails may use powerful magnetic motors to speed along.

Pantograph
The folding power collection device used on many electric trains. The pantograph unfolds from the top of the locomotive to touch against power cables suspended above the track. Other types of electric train can use power collectors mounted underneath the locomotive. These rub against a third, centre rail, to pick up the electricity supply.

Spike

Fixing pin which joins a rail to a sleeper. There are many different designs, but they all do the same basic job. For joining rails end-on, metal fixing sections called fishplates are used.

Streamlined

A train which is specially-shaped to cut through the air, smoothly and cleanly. Normally, the front end of a streamlined locomotive is designed in flowing curves, which push through the air more easily than flat, blunt shapes. Streamlining is necessary only for high speed though: only then does air resistance become a major force. For really fast trains, designers try to make *everything* smoother – wheels are covered over, doors and windows made flush with coach sides and so on. Streamlining is not new – in the 1930s, many express trains had sleek loco-motives pulling them.

Tender

Wagon which carries a steam locomotive's water and fuel. The fuel is usually coal, though wood or oil can be used. Tank engines carry their own water and fuel supplies, and are named for the tanks in which the water is stored.

Traction motor

Name for the powerful electric motors used to propel an electric locomotive.

Trackway

Name for early guided lines before the system of using metal rails was developed. Channels were dug into the ground to act as grooves for wheeled trucks. Almost all early trackways (and the first railways) were built for use in mines, to carry out material from the tunnels in which minerals, such as coal or iron, were removed.

Wheel code

Also known as the Whyte notation, it describes the number and type of wheels on a steam locomotive. Other codes are used to describe the wheel arrangements of diesel and electric locomotives.

△ The picture shows the principle of the steam locomotive, here shown on a wood-burning American type 4-4-0 of the 1870s. A furnace (**1**) heats water contained in the boiler (**2**). High-pressure steam (**3**) from the boiler passes from the dome (**4**) through tubes (**5**) to the cylinder (**6**), where it pushes a piston (**7**) back and forth. The piston is joined by connecting rods (**8**) to the driving wheels (**9**), making them turn, so driving the locomotive along the track.

A multiple-tube arrangement from the firebox into the boiler makes heating water quicker and more efficient.

Index

A WORLD OF FESTIVALS

CHINESE NEW YEAR

Catherine Chambers

Evans Brothers Limited

Published by Evans Brothers Limited
2A Portman Mansions
Chiltern Street
London W1M 1LE

© copyright Evans Brothers Limited 1997

British Library Cataloguing in Publication data.
A catalogue record for this book is available from the
British Library.

First published 1997

Printed in Spain by G.Z. Printek

0 237 51672 1

ACKNOWLEDGEMENTS

Editor: Su Swallow
Design: Neil Sayer
Production: Jenny Mulvanny

For permission to reproduce copyright material, the
author and publishers gratefully acknowledge the following:

Cover Liba Taylor/Hutchison Library
Title page Chapman Lee/Image Bank
page 6 Robert Harding Picture Library **page 7** (top)
Robert Harding Picture Library (bottom) Chris
Stowers/Panos Pictures **page 8** (background) Sally
and Richard Greenhill (foreground) Trip/H Rogers
page 10 Robert Harding Picture Library **page 11**
Chapman Lee/Image Bank **page 12** Trip/J Wakelin
page 13 (top) Mary Evans Picture Library (bottom)
Robert Harding Picture Library **page 14** Emma
Lee/Life File **page 15** Juliet Highet/Life File **page 17**
(top) Maurice Harvey/Hutchison Library (bottom)
Margaret Collier/Robert Harding Picture Library
page 18 Sarah Murray/Hutchison Library **page 19**
Guido Rossi/Image Bank **page 20** G. Corrigan/
Robert Harding Picture Library **page 21** (top)
Martha Cooper/Viesti Associate, Inc. (bottom)
Robert Harding Picture Library **page 23** (top right)
Trip/A Tovey (middle) Zefa **page 24** Sarah
Murray/Hutchison Library **page 25** Jeremy
Hoare/Life File **page 26** (top) Joseph Brignola/Image
Bank (bottom) Mary Evans Picture Library **page 27**
Trip/J Moscrop **page 28/29** Alan Towse Photography
page 30 Paul Van Riel/Robert Harding Picture
Library